EXPLORING INNER SPACE

The voyage of self-discovery

by

Frank MacHovec PhD

FOREWORD

Canadian psychiatrist Eric Berne was once asked what he thought best reflected good mental health. He said the answers to three basic questions were likely to mean someone is mentally healthy:

1. Who are you?
2. Who are these other people around and near you?
3. What the hell are you doing?

This book is to help you answer those questions. It is a distillation of many courses and workshops given throughout the U.S. and Canada for 25 years. Each chapter is based on one of those three basic questions which then become:

1. Who are you?
   Self-awareness and introspection.

2. Who are these other people?
   Interpersonal communications and group dynamics.

3. What the hell are you doing?
    Problem solving, decision making,
    coping with difficult people and
    situations.

    There is a 4th chapter on keeping well, to
help you manage stress. This book is not a
substitute for therapy though it can help you
benefit from therapy and adjust to your life
situation. If anything in this book is
upsetting to you, consult a licensed mental
health professional.

    Welcome to the human race, a very
special life form in a vast and lonely
universe. Come with me now to explore
your inner space -- and become a
psychonaut!

CONTENTS

1
WHO ARE YOU?
Self-awareness

> Make the most of yourself.
> That's all there is of you!
> -- Ralph Waldo Emerson

This book is aimed at helping you answer three basic questions posed years ago by Canadian psychiatrist Eric Berne:

1. Who are you? Self-awareness; identity; introspection.
2. Who are these others? Interpersonal relations; group dynamics.
3. What the hell are you doing? Problem solving, decision making, coping with difficult people.

The first three chapters will help you answer those questions and a fourth chapter will help you manage stress. This book is a basic training manual for exploring inner space, the voyage of self-discovery. By reading and studying it you will qualify as a *Psychonaut First Class!*

ORIENTATION

We begin, like learning to fly, with "ground school," realizing that where you are and where you live have an effect on your behavior. Your surroundings, big city or rural area, what you do for a living, how you spend time, your friends and fellow workers or classmates, even what you eat and when, influence behavior. They vary from one person to another. Those factors and more help shape you into a one-of-a-kind unique individual.

Historians debate whether it is the *time* or the *person* that shape leaders. It's likely both are significant forces. As Thomas Paine wrote: "These are the times that try men's souls" and in *The Tale of Two Cities* Charles Dickens wrote: "It was the best of times, it was the worst of times." But Dickens also wrote: "A wonderful fact to reflect on is that every human creature is a profound secret and mystery to every other" Differences can be enriching. In fact, you can learn as much if not more from those who differ with you.

THE WORLD OF PSYCHOLOGY

Psychology is *the science of behavior and mental processes,* so it is useful to begin with considering what psychology is – and isn't.

It's a strange word, rooted in the legend of Psyche. She was the most beautiful human and as such she was noticed and envied by Aphrodite (or Venus), the goddess of beauty. She sent her son Eros (or Cupid) to earth to cast a spell on Psyche with one of his golden arrows so she would fall in love with the ugliest, meanest human. However, when Eros saw her it was love at first sight and they ran away together. For years they wandered the earth and suffered greatly. Aphrodite eventually took pity on them and transformed Psyche into a goddess.

Psychology was originally a branch of philosophy. The highest academic degree is still the PhD -- doctor of philosophy -- though few psychologists take even one course in philosophy. There is also a PsyD: doctor of psychology. It's based on more hours of clinical training to prepare for a licensed mental health profession. Psychology is a science because it imposes the strict discipline of *the scientific method* shared by all the sciences:

1. State the purpose, intent, goal
2. Observe objectively, what's there not what you want to see
3. Gather data, omit nothing
4. Evaluate, let the data take you where it Will
5. Conclude, which should emerges of and by itself
6. Refine, by replication (repeating) to further refine the conclusion -- a feedback loop

There are *unscientific methods* such as astrology, palmistry, and unscientific ways to explain behavior, such as **m**yth, superstition, preconceived notions, half truth, personal bias, and stereotyping. Here's sample. Which are *valid generalizations* and which are unscientific?

1. Blondes have more fun.
2. It always rains on vacation.
3. Muslims are terrorists.
4. Speed kills.
5. Practice makes perfect.

It may be every blonde you ever knew were fun to be with, but that is insufficient data to conclude all blondes have more fun. That is a universal that means all blondes who ever lived and who will ever live were, are, or will have more fun. There's no way you can know that. It may be that it rained on every vacation you've ever taken, but you can't predict that it will *always* rain on your vacation. Only a small fraction of the world's millions of Muslims are terrorists. There may be a time when a burst of speed can avoid an accident. If you do not have the aptitude or training for a skill, practice will not guarantee perfection. So, none of those statements are ***valid generalizations***.

The scientific way to rephrase those statements would add words such as:

1. Every blonde I have ever known had more fun.
2. It has rained during every vacation for the past ten years.
3. Some Muslim extremists are terrorists.
4. Excessive speed increases the risk losing control.
5. If you are talented, practice is likely to help you improve that specific skill.

A fairly common unscientific way to describe behavior is the *fallacy of exception,* such as: "My grandfather chain smoked cigars and live to be 100, so smoking isn't a bad health risk." Your grandfather was an exception. There are thousands of cases of emphysema and lung cancer directly linked to smoking and even from second-hand smoke. An exception is just that, and it's dangerous to assume you will escape the consequences that apply to thousands of others who did not. In war-time, soldiers have joked that they don't worry about the bullet with their name on it but the one labeled "to whom it may concern."

There is a substantial body of data to justify *valid generalizations.* For example, we know now that even eyewitness testimony can be unreliable. Memory o an event can vary from one person to another. If hypnosis is used to "refresh memory" it fixes it. So, if the memory was faulty before, it will be moreso, and remain so after hypnosis. Bottom line: hypnotically refreshed testimony is no longer admissible in most courts.

Let's return to psychonaut training. There are areas where psychology is not yet able to precisely define some traits despite decades of research. Examples: personality, intelligence, memory, and hypnosis. We know a great deal about all of them but we do not have universally accepted definitions of any of them. To explore inner space you need to know five basic personality theories. Here they are, oldest to most recent:

TYPOLOGIES AND TRAITS

This is the oldest personality theory and dates back to Hippocrates, a priest-physician in the cult of Asklepios on the island of Kos in 300 BCE. He also classified illness as to acute or chronic, mild, moderate, or severe, and his admonition "do no harm" is still the criterion in malpractice and negligence 2300 years later. He taught four basic personality types: sanguine, choleric, melancholic, and phlegmatic, based on organ function. Ivan Pavlov found four basic personalities in his research with dogs. Carl Jung believed that there are three basic personality dynamics, each on a sliding scale: extroversion to introversion, sensing and perceiving, and thinking and feeling. Isabel Myers-Briggs added judging-intuiting. This ancient theory is alive and well in psychology's newest personality theory called 5-factor theory of five basic traits: openness to new experiences, conscientiousness, extroversion, agreeableness, and neuroticism (later changed to emotional stability). **Bottom line**: It takes all kinds. **Goal**: Realize your type and traits.

PSYCHOANALYTIC-PSYCHODYNAMIC

This is the personality theory described by Sigmund Freud. He described the mind as much like an iceberg, most of its content submerged, beyond reach, and he called the unknown part the unconscious. The basic life force is the *libido*, in two parts: *eros*, positive and life sustaining, and *thanatos*, negative and destructive, "the death wish. There are three *ego states* co-existent in everyone: the *id*, the primitive pleasure-seeking self from birth; *ego*, the reality principle and mediator emerging at about age 1; and the *superego*, conscience and values, an internalized parent, at about age 3. Freud said: "Ego and id are like rider and horse. Often the rider guides the horse where it itself wants to go. Where there is id that is where ego should be."

Freud saw personality as developing through five *ego stages* beginning with the *oral stage* the proceeding through *anal, phallic, latency,* **and** *genital.* Someone can be *fixated* at any stage, such as a pedophile who then seeks victims in that stage.

Defense mechanisms protect the ego from painful reality. Freud called dreams "the royal road to the unconscious and interpreting them is a way to see into the unconscious mind. Based on 1000 dreams, he suggested that dreams are: triggered by events of the preceding 24 hours, usually cleverly disguised and symbolic, and "the fulfiller of wishes." When waking the superego blocks memory, so Freud recommended keeping a notepad at bedside to quickly note dream content which is *manifest* obvious "window dressing," and *latent,* the disguised *real meaning.* Common dream themes: falling, lost, running, swimming, climbing, naked, surgery. A *lucid dream* is one in which you are aware you're dreaming. **Bottom line:** You're a monkey's uncle. **Goal:** Free the ego.

Freud's therapy was historical, always going back from a present problem to the last time it occurred, eventually to the earliest occurrence. He called it *anamnesis,* and when he found the original source he helped the patient relive it, vent it, thus neutralizing it. He called that *abreaction* and *working through*. It has helped crime victims, survivors of catastrophes, and war veterans. Hypnosis has also helped. After achieving a good hypnotic level, traumas are relived when hypnotized, then the memory blocked until the patient is strong enough to recall the event without hypnosis.

Freud hoped Swiss psychiatrist Carl Jung would succeed him, but Jung left to form his own theoretical school. Jung further refined Freud's unconscious by adding the *collective unconscious,* common mental and dream imagery shared across time and cultures. He found that people worldwide had similar dream imagery regardless of language and culture he called them *primordial archetypes*. Jung also gave us the *persona* or public face such as police officer, doctor, store clerk, etc. and the *shadow*, a person within you opposite to your thoughts or feelings, kind of Dr. Jekyll and Mr. Hyde.

Alfred Adler was an ophthalmologist accepted in Freud's inner circle who originated the *compensation* defense mechanism, that you are likely to try to make up for some real or imagined deficiency. He based it on the finding that one eye will compensate for a weaker eye. Adler also suggested superiority and inferiority complexes and the effect of birth order, your placement in the family, youngest, oldest, middle, or only child.

Melanie Klein was one of the first women to get an MD degree and one of the very few accepted in Freud's inner circle and weekly meetings. After Freud's death she had serious differences with Anna Freud, the only one of Freud's six children who became a mental health professional and preserved Freud's legacy in the Vienna Psychoanalytic Society. Klein suggested the mother bond with children was a stronger force than father-child. Well, the father figure in the Oedipus complex was strict dogma that Anna Freud vehemently defended. The

Viennese Psychoanalytic Society sided with Anna Freud. Klein's theory, called *object relations,* is now a popular trend in psychoanalysis, strengthened by the *attachment theory* of John Bowlby and Mary Ainsworth.

Another gifted woman was Karen Horney (pronounced horn-eye, please!), a Berlin MD also accepted into Freud's inner circle. She described *four selves* co-existing in the personality: *reputational, idealized, personal,* and *real.* She also described how excessive demands and exaggerated needs become neurotic extremes. Her books are easily read and can be found at used book websites.

A psychoanalyst of note was the Berlin psychologist Erich Fromm. Like most of Freud's colleagues and like Freud himself, Fromm fled from Nazi Germany but witnessed the rise of Nazism and how the German people reacted to it. His book *Escape from freedom* describes it and remains timely, applicable to various similar nationalistic movements that have become violent. Fromm and Horney are increasingly referred to as examples of *sociocultural personality theory.*

BEHAVIORISM

New York psychologist John B. Watson reacted to Freud with irritation and anger. To Watson, Freud's ideas could not be tested by experiment. They were based on individual case studies by Freud and his followers. Watson boldly stated: "Give me a dozen healthy infants and my own specialized world and I'll take any one at random and train them to become any type of specialist: doctor, lawyer, artist, merchant, and yes, beggar man or thief."

He claimed all behavior is learned and conditioned and that only "overt, observable behavior" was appropriate for research and theory. Hence, this movement became *behaviorism.* Later, Ivan Pavlov's work with dogs, bells, and salivation, called *classical conditioning,* strengthened this approach. B.F. Skinner applied it to more complicated behaviors, like driving a car, using a drink machine, or ATM. He called it *operant conditioning.*

The seeds of behaviorism go back to the British mathematician-philosopher John Locke who claimed that personality is learned, shaped by everything that happens after one's birth. He described a newborn's mind as a blank slate, a *tabula rasa*. Currently, behavorist concepts are used in behavior modification, systematic desensitization of phobias, and cognitive-behavioral therapy. **Bottom line:** You've been shaped. **Goal**: Optimize adaptive coping.

10 COGNITIVE DISTORTIONS
(Neff, 1985)

1. **Perfectionism**. *Antidote*: be reasonable.
2. **Rejectionitis,** exaggerating deficiencies. *Antidote*: make a positives checklist.
3. **Negativism**. *Antidote*: choose to be positive.
4. **Refusing positives.** *Antidote*: say "thanks" -- nothing more.
5. **White-is-black,** seeing positives negatively. *Antidote*: **be** realistic.
6. **Stretch-or-shrink.** maximizing negatives, minimizing positives. *Antidote*: Reality!

7. **Fictional fantasy,** off-the-wall unreality. *Antidote*: objective fact!
8. **Should-ought-must.** *Antidote:* be reasonable.
9. **Mistaken identity,** such as belief you're a bad person. *Antidote:* it's OK to make mistakes.
10. **Over-apologizing.** *Antidote:* accept responsibility, express concern -- then move on!

12 DISTRESSING MYTHS
(Roberts and Guttormson, 1990)
1. You must be loved by everyone and everyone must love everything you do.
2. You must be competent and intelligent in everything you do.
3. Some things are evil and wrong and you must be punished for thinking or doing them.
4. All is lost when things don't turn out the way you want them to.
5. You have no control over happiness. It depends solely on what happens to you.
6. Worrying keeps whatever's bad from happening.

7. It's always easier to run away from problems than deal with them.
8. You need someone else to depend on. You can't function well independently.
9. Anything bad that happens will affect you forever.
10. If anyone isn't how you think he or she should be, you must try to change them.
11. There is only one correct answer to any problem and the consequences are terrible if that one answer isn't found.
12. You can't ever help or change how you feel.

HUMANISTIC PSYCHOLOGY

A group of American psychologists grew dissatisfied with Freud's psychoanalytic theory and Watson's behaviorism that to them were both fatalistic (deterministic). If Freud was right, you are driven by instinct. If Watson was right, you are shaped by whatever happens to you. Either way you're a victim. If the traits and types theory is true, what's inside you are like cards dealt you at conception. These rebellious psychologists called themselves *humanistic* because they believed in individual differences, that a person can overcome or control instinctive drives, environmental forces, or personal traits. This is the unique contribution of humanistic psychology to education and personality theory. It has stimulated alternative therapies such as meditation, mindfulness, massage, and other innovative alternative treatments that became part of *transpersonal psychology.*

All the classic personality theories have deep roots in history and philosophy. Just as traits and types go back to Hippocrates and perhaps even before, Freud's emphasis on drive states go back to Darwin and before. Watson's approach extended Locke's blank slate (tabula rasa) and humanistic psychologists applied what was theorized much earlier. Jean Jacques Rousseau in Geneva wrote that "everything is good when it leaves the hands of the Creator." He spoke highly of Native Americans at a time many referred to them as savages. Rousseau said that if they were savages they were *noble savages.*

Rousseau and earlier philosophers such as Socrates who urged students to "know thyself," helped sow the seeds of what became a humanistic deep respect for the dignity and integrity of the individual. Two influential humanistic psychologists were Carl Rogers who emphasized *empathy* and *unconditional positive regard,* and Abraham Maslow who formulated *five universal needs,* the highest being *self-actualization.* **Bottom line:** Everyone is unique. Personality is more becoming than being, a continuing process of personal growth. **Goal:** Become!

MASLOW'S UNIVERSAL NEEDS

Level 1: SURVIVAL. Air, food, and water and to be warm and dry, the universal dependency of infancy.

Level 2: SECURITY. Shelter, safety, free from external danger, a need from early childhood.

Level 3: SUPPORT. The "apron strings stage" of early and middle childhood and similar emotional support later.

Level 4: **SELF-ESTEEM.** Fellow feeling, acceptance, belonging, team spirit, teens to adulthood.

Level 5: **SELF-ACTUALIZATION.** Personal fulfillment, achievement, and realizing your potential.

SELF-ACTUALIZATION
Maslow studied successful well-adjusted people to discover how they differed from others. He found personality traits he called *B-values* (B for becoming), healthy traits of self-actualized people we can emulate:
1. **TRUTH** more than dishonesty, distrust, cynicism, or disbelief.
2. **GOOD, GOODNESS** more than evil, hate, selfishness, or negativism.
3. **BEAUTY, ELEGANCE** more than vulgarity, ugliness, being clumsy or shoddy.
4. **UNITY, WHOLENESS** rather than arbitrariness, disorganization, fragmentation, or needless nit-picking.
5. **VITALITY, LIVELINESS** more than dull, empty, or "emotionless robotism."

6. **UNIQUENESS** rather than monotony or lack of individuality.
7. **COMPLETION** rather than imperfection, futility, or apathy.
8. **ORDER, ORDERLINESS** more than chaos, tension, or disorganization.
9. **SIMPLICITY** rather than complexity, confusion, conflict.
10. **EFFORTLESSNESS**, "easy does it" rather than tedium, rigidity, or strain.
11. **HUMOR** and **PLAYFULNESS** instead of being stuffy, pretentious, or distrusting.
12. **SELF-SUFFICIENCY** rather than overdependence or insecurity.
13. **MEANING** more than meaninglessness, emptiness, or futility.
14. **JUSTICE, FAIRNESS** rather than injustice, unfairness, and insecurity.

SICK NEEDS

Karen Horney formulated a list of **neurotic needs**:

1. *Excessive* affection and/or approval
2. *Excessive* (total) dependency
3. *Excessive* need to narrowly limit goals
4. *Excessive* power or control
5. *Excessive* need to exploit others

6. *Excessive* recognition or praise
7. *Excessive* need for personal admiration
8. *Excessive* need achievement and exclusivity
9. *Excessive* independence and self-sufficiency (no commitments)
10. *Excessive* need for perfection (invulnerability)

You may have a *tendency* toward one or more these sick needs. A *tendency* is normal. *Excess* is not. Needs become abnormal, sick, when they are *excessive* and *extreme*. Many people are misunderstood because a healthy need may seem excessive to others.

6 WAYS TO WEAKEN EFFECTIVENESS
(Karen Horney)

1. **Relentless demands** such as overdoing, seeing your best work as not good enough, or unrealistic expectations of others.
2. **Merciless self-accusation** such as excessively blaming yourself for whatever goes wrong, exaggerated self-criticism.
3. **Self-contempt** such as low self-esteem, when you really don't like yourself.

4. **High frustration level** such as impatience, intolerance, overacting, having "a short fuse."
5. **Masochistic self-torment** such as putting yourself down or failing to recognize and realize anything good you achieve.
6. **Self-destructive behavior** such as a pattern of failure in friendships, love, career, alcohol or drug abuse (includes smoking), or being accident prone.

SOCIOCULTURAL THEORY

Erich Fromm, Karen Horney, and similar thinkers emphasized social interaction and culture as important forces that shape personality. Cultural diversity training is an example of attempts to overcome prejudice and stereotyping and to show differences need not be divisive but challenging, even enriching. Evidence of this is the continuing popularity of ethnic and nationalistic foods such as Chinese, Mexican, Indian, and other restaurants.

German sociologists contributed to socioculutral personality theory with terms such as *Weltanschauung* (one's world view), *Zeitgeist* (the spirit of the time), *Gemein-*

schaft (small town informality), and *Gesellschaft* (big city anonymity). French philosophers added *anomie* (isolation, alienation), *joie de vivre* (joy of/in life), and *elan vital* (spiritedness). **Bottom line:** Culture is a force. **Goal**: Appreciate differences and strive to realize universal ethics and values.

EXERCISE. Which of the five classic personality theories do you think best describes human nature and personality? All five reflect some truth but none of them is all-true, so if you exclude any of them renders personality incomplete. Your preference should tell you a lot about your own personality dynamics. Think about it.

FORCES THAT SHAPE PERSONALITY

Let's take a closer look at force s that shaped personality:

1. **Genetic traits and predispositions,** gifts of nature, how you're wired, the cards dealt you at conception
2. **Ethnicity** includes race, national origin, religion, and culture

3. **Community**, group identity, social status.
4. **Home and family.** Parents are your first teachers and according to Melanie Klein, the mother-bond sets the tone for all future relationships.
5. **Friends.** Ralph Waldo Emerson said: "Show me your friends and I will know who you are."
6. **Education.** School years were your first forced socialization and gradual personal and intellectual growth)
7. **Work.** Kahlil Gibran wrote: "Love what you do and do what you love"

EXERCISE. Go over these seven forces. What effect did each have on you? How much was positive? How much was negative? Anything you can do to neutralize the negatives and improve on the positives?

In his book *Taproots*, Bill O'Hanlon described this realization process:
To *realize* you need *real eyes*
to see *real lies* and be able to say:
"Real I is!"
(ungrammatical but true)

MULTIPLE INTELLIGENCES

Harvard psychology professor Howard Gardner wrote: "I put forth intelligences as a new definition of human nature." He added: "Socrates saw man as a rational animal. Freud stressed the irrationality of human beings. I (with due tentativeness) have described human beings as organisms who possess a basic set of seven, eight, or a dozen intelligences." He described them as "potentials we can mobilize and connect according to our own inclination and our culture's preferences." Here's his original formulation:

Two intelligences "typically valued in school"

LINGUISTIC: "Sensitivity to spoken and written language, ability to learn and use language, such as lawyers, writers, poets, therapists, and politicians.

LOGICAL-MATHEMATICAL: "Capacity to analyze problems logically, carry out mathematical operations, and investigate issues scientifically." Mathematicians, theo-ologians, and scientists. "Most psychologists and other academics exhibit an amalgam of linguistic and mathematical intelligence that made it inevitable those faculties dominated tests of intelligence." Three intelligences "particularly notable in the arts"

MUSICAL: "Skill in the performance, composition, and appreciation of musical patterns...almost parallel structurally to linguistic intelligence and it makes neither scientific nor logical sense to call one (usually linguistic) an intelligence and the other (usually musical) a talent."

BODY-KINESTHETIC: "Using one's body to solve problems or fashion products such as dancers, actors, athletes, craftspersons, surgeons, bench-top scientists, mechanics, and technically oriented professionals."

SPATIAL: "To recognize and manipulate space such as navigators and pilots as well as more confined areas like sculptors, surgeons, chess players, graphic artists, and architects. Different cultures show how biopsychological potential can be harnessed and evolved for a variety of purposes."

Two "personal intelligences"

INTERPERSONAL: "Capacity to understand intentions, motivations, and desires and consequently work effectively with others." Therapists, teachers, salespeople, clergy, politicians, actors.

INTRAPERSONAL: "Capacity to understand oneself, have an effective working model of oneself including desires, fears, capacities, and use it effectively in regulating one's own life. I consider emotional factors of each intelligence rather than restricting emotions to one or two intelligences. Recent evolutionary and psychological research stresses the history of interpersonal intelligence as compared to the relatively recent emergence of intrapersonal intelligence.

Three possible others

NATURALIST: "Expertise in the recognition and classification of the numerous species, flora and fauna." Examples: Aristotle, Linneaus, Darwin, Agassiz, and Audubon.

EXISTENTIAL: "The potential to engage in transcendental concerns...the capacity to locate oneself ...to the furthest reaches of the cosmos, the infinite and infinitesimal and the related capacity, the significance of life, the meaning of death, the ultimate fate of the physical and psychological worlds...love of another person or total immersion in a work of art...without attaining an ultimate truth."

SPIRITUAL: "A desire to know about experiences and cosmic entities not readily apprehended in a material sense but nonetheless important to human beings. If we can relate to the world of nature we can also relate to the supernatural world, to the cosmos that extends beyond what we perceive directly, to the mystery of our own existence, and to life-and-death experiences that transcend what we routinely encounter...regrettably, the majority of scholars in the cognitive and behavioral sciences turn away from questions of a spiritual nature. It is primarily phenomenological, beyond cognitive investigation." In 2000 Gardner questioned whether there is a spiritual intelligence and suggested it may just be a variation of existential intelligence. One wonders if Camus, Sartre, Heidegger, Husserl, and other existentialists would agree!

SKILL BUILDERS

1. *You are free. Define yourself!* This was a classic statement from Europe's existentialist philosophers. Without using your name, age, gender, politics, religion, race, or national origin, describe who you are in as many ways you can. It isn't easy! Artists, poets, composers, and philosophers spend lives reflecting on this aspect of identity. Even those troubled, like Van Gogh and Lautrec showed their "search for self" in their work.

2. *Your favorites.* Make a list:
   (a) food   (d) drink   (g) sport
   (b) movie   (e) actor   (h) dessert
   (c) car   (f) music   (i) color
            (j) leisure activity
If you asked others, would you expect their answers to be the same as yours? Unlikely. This exercise proves there are individual

differences and that everyone is a unique individual.

3. *Factors that shape personality.* Go over the list of factors. How have they influenced your behavior? There is a negative potential if they interfere with healthy personality development. Then, you could become defensive or feel inferior. Is there anything in them that may prevent you from becoming the best *you*?

4. *Media spin and loose talk.* Print and TV advertising, news and talk shows, political campaigns, and overheard conversations are opportunities to detect slanting and misperception. Use them to sharpen your perception and separate fact from distortion. Ernest Hemingway was asked the most useful writer's skill. He replied: "A 100% effective BS detector!" Tune yours up!

5. *Maslow's needs hierarchy.* How can you help others meet their needs, such as a (a) friend; (b) parent; (c) neighbor; (d) classmate or coworker; (e) fellow citizen?

6. *Sick needs.* How can you ensure any sick needs or demands you have won't interfere with life and work? Think of examples you have seen and use them as lessons of how not to behave. Observe TV personalities. Does their behavior suggest any neurotic needs?

7. *Self-actualization.* Review and reflect on the B-values and rate yourself on a 3-point scale: 3 (high level), 2 (average but could do more), or 1 (low and need much more). How can you reach and maintain higher levels?

9. *Personality theories.* Earlier you were asked which personality theory you think best describes human nature? To choose only one or omit any of them gives an incomplete description of personality. None is 100% true but there is some truth in each of them.

RECOMMENDED READING

Cross, J. & Cross, P.B. (2005). *Knowing yourself inside out.* Berkeley CA: Crystal Publications. www.crystalpublications.net od self-test based on Carl Jung's typologies:

Keirsey, D., and Bates, M. *Please under-stand me" Character and temperament types.* Del Mar CA: Prometheus Nemesis Books. (A good self-test based on Carl Jung's typologies)

PARTING THOUGHTS

I do my thing and you do your thing. I am not in this world to live up to your expectations and you are not in this world to live up to mine. You are you and I am I. If by chance we find each other, that's beautiful. If not, it can't be helped.
-- Fritz Perls
(founder of Gestalt therapy)

God, grant me the serenity to accept what cannot be changed, the courage to change what should be changed and the wisdom to know the difference.
(attributed to St. Francis of Assisi)

2
WHO ARE THESE
OTHER PEOPLE?
Interpersonal awareness

> All the world is queer
> save me and thee, and
> I think thee are a little
> queer.
> -- old Quaker saying

LISTENING SKILLS

THE ARC METHOD

ARC stands for **A**ttention, **R**eflection, and **C**larification.

A = ATTENTION

... sets the stage for effective listening, an open, receptive, attitude, without judging or concluding, just hearing what is said. The goal is to hear what is said not what you want to hear or would like to hear. A sign of this step is *following behavior*: a nod, eye contact, a smile, leaning a bit toward the speaker, and acknowledging words such as "Uh-uh...yes...I see..." etc.

R = REFLECTION

... is the most frequently omitted and when it is it almost always results in mis-understanding. The goal is *not* to react to what has been said, to debate, even agree or disagree, but to show you really understand what was said by reflecting or mirroring it *in your own words*. Signs of it are neutral body language (especially face and eyes), calm tone of voice, neutral language ("I hear you saying..." or your own *neutral* response). Avoid: "Do you mean...are you saying..." These statements can sound antagonistic.

C = CLARIFICATION

... is when the person who spoke first acknowledges and confirms you understood what was said and, if needed, refines it -- *still without taking sides*. It's a final assurance the intended message is understood. The person who spoke accepts or corrects the reflection of the listener. *After* clarification both sides can agree, differ, or discuss the matter further.

BODY LANGUAGE

Body language, also called nonverbal behavior or *kinesics*, is the way posture, placement, and movements show attitude, thoughts, and feelings. **A word of caution:** you can read too much in another person's body language just as it is also possible to miss an important useful clue. Most of us have favorite ways of sitting, standing, even walking. Some can feel anxious but appear relaxed. Still, there are some research-based generalizations about body language. It can be…

… **learned** from parents, others, or yourself

as a habit.

… an **unconscious reflex** like a startle

reaction or eye blink.

… a **conscious choice** like waving, pointing,

or shrugging.

… **role or situational behavior** such as
directing someone or a police officer
directing traffic.

MAJOR FEATURES

Position and posture: *Where* and *how* you sit, stand, and walk.

Place behavior: The setting such as a party, church, beach, library, school, or restaurant.

Personal space: The physical and psychological distance between you, pets, kids, friends, coworkers, boss, others.

Gesture: *Signals* given by hand or finger(s).

Incidence: *How frequently* it happens.

Intensity and range of motion: the *force* of movement and *how far* such as a nod, waving a hand, etc.

Face and head signals: involvement of forehead, eyebrows, eyelids, eyes, mouth, lips, tongue, cheeks (most accurate according to experts).

Costume: Uniform or clothing, its design, color, and fit.

Ornamentation: Rings, pins, tattoos, etc.

Props such as tools, clipboard, briefcase, files, forms, book, manual.

Bottom line: Human behavior is complex. Don't oversimplify or jump to conclusions.

DEFENSE MECHANISMS

In stressful situations beyond our control we sometimes cope by using *defense mechanisms*. Freud said they are rooted in the unconscious mind below conscious awareness. They are automatic, like a boxer with guard up defending against blows that might come at any moment. We're unaware we use them unless someone points them out or we become aware we are over-reacting. Defense mechanisms you may see in yourself and others:

1. ACTING OUT is impulsive behavior such as losing self-control and over-reacting by with an outburst of temper, angrily walking out, swearing, or trashing things.

2. AVOIDANCE: refusal or inability to acknowledge a problem. We also avoid by:

DENIAL or **SUPPRESSION. DENIAL** is failing to take personal responsibility for an obvious reactions or attitude. Example: loudly exclaiming: "Who's angry? Not me!" or a tearful: "Oh, that's all right, it was nothing."

SUPPRESSION is a *conscious choice* to avoid a problem, person, or situation. Example: Scarlett O'Hara (Vivien Leigh) in the movie *Gone with the Wind* saying: "I'm not going t think of it. Tomorrow is another day."

3. EXTERNALIZATION, blaming others or other circumstance for your own shortcomings. Example: "If it weren't for ___ I would have gotten it done." There are several varieties:

DISPLACEMENT: "dumping" anger or frustration on someone or something not involved in the problem or situation. It is also called "flypaper syndrome" since to get rid of irritation you stick it on to someone or something else rather than getting at the real problem cause.

ISOLATION is to "nit-pick," exaggerating a minor problem, "making a mountain out of a molehill." It's rushing to judgment with too few facts. Example: "Air bags are dangerous. They kill babies." But doing away with them would kill many more men, women, and children than the infants who died from them.

PROJECTION is like shining a flashlight (projecting) on others, falsely blaming them for your own thoughts or feelings. Example: "That office spends too much time socializing" can really mean: "I'd like to take time to have fun, too."

4. EXAGGERATION is *distorting* reality such as:

DISCOUNTING or **DEVALUING**, is "putting down" someone or something or "badmouthing" a person or problem.

IDEALIZATION or **HALO EFFECT** is exaggerating a person's positive behaviors or traits out of realistic proportion, such as hero worship and fan clubs. It's normal to admire people and consider them role models but not to exaggerate their positive qualities so much no one could equal them.

5. SMOKE SCREEN is defending yourself by "blowing smoke" in words or actions that confuse and keep people at a distance. There are two kinds:

INTELLECTUALIZING, also known as "double talk, word salad, head tripping, or BS," is using technical jargon or abstract ideas, trivia or tangents with little or no relevance to the problem or subject at hand.

RATIONALIZING is explaining away a problem. Robert Louis Stevenson said: "I've heard many excuses but not one good reason."

6. PASSIVE-AGGRESSIVE BEHAVIOR, also called foot dragging, dogging it, or sand bagging, is being a passive obstructionist. Example: The old saying: "You can lead a horse to water but you can't make it drink." Or when you do not intervene to prevent a problem you saw coming."

7. HUMOR is a healthy defense if used as an icebreaker to overcome distance or brush away embarrassment, or in lighthearted needling if used positively. It is negative and destructive when it avoids reality, hurts others, or distances you from a problem or reality.

8. REACTION FORMATION is responding opposite to your real feelings, such as remaining aloof or distant from a neighbor, friend, or coworker you like but avoid getting closer.

9. UNDOING is overdoing, over-reacting to conceal your true feelings.

INTERACTING!

Transactional analysis or TA is a system of analyzing interactions created by Eric Berne MD, a Canadian psychiatrist.

STROKES are anything said or done to another person. There are three kinds:
1. **Warm fuzzies**, expressing real, positive thoughts and feelings.
2. **Cold pricklies**, antagonistic or demeaning thoughts or feelings.
3. **Plastic fuzzies**, artificial, phony expressions.

STATES. There are three coexisting parts of you, also in everyone else:

Child (C) who "comes on" at birth and is where all your *feelings* are

Parent (P) comes on by age 5 by which time 25,000 hours of tapes have played in you from real-life parents

Adult (A) comes on by age 1 and *mediates* between your *Parent* and your *Child*

TRANSACTIONS are exchanges of strokes to and from your Parent, Adult, or Child and any of those in another person. There is a + and – Parent, + when reassuring, supportive or – when blaming, demeaning. + Parents say: "Great...you're doing fine...you're OK" etc. - Parents say: "I told you so...I'm not surprised...some day you'll thank me." There is a + and – Child (or Kid). The OK Kid feels "up." The Not OK Kid feels "down." Not OK Kids say "I can't...won't...do I have to...I don't wanna" etc. OK Kids say "neat...cool...let's...can I..." etc. Having fun is between two OK Kids. The Adult asks questions, explores alternatives, decides, manages, and mediates between Parent and Child. Transactions can be analyzed by drawing arrows from and to P, A, or C:

P	P
A	A
C	C
You	*Other person*

Be aware of negative transactions. Here are two:

1. You're standing at a bus stop in the rain. The person next to you says: "Another bad day." You say: "Yeah, and I want to go downtown for the 1-day sale at X *Store.*" The other person says: "They won't have half the stuff. They just advertise to get you in the store." "Yeah," you add, "and even if they did, the sales clerks don't now where it is." This is an exchange of cold prickly strokes called **Ain't it awful.** It can end with your blaming Parent in a bad mood all day. The antidote is to deliver the punch line: "It's really awful." If the other person continues anyway, just repeat that closing kiss-off.

2. You get out of your new car just as your neighbor stands nearby. You comment:

"This is a new Super Pooper, the first one delivered." Your neighbor says: "Really? I just bought a Bammo Bombo and it's the only one made so far." You say: "My car has an engine in the trunk I can run in an emergency." Neighbor: "Mine has eight wheels, a pair at each corner." You say: "Mine has 36 speakers and a 30" woofer." This is an exchange of cold pricklies between two malicious little kids and it's called **Mine's better'n yours**. It's often played about cars, homes, neighborhoods, jobs, sports, spouses, political candidates, race, religions, and nationalities. Chances are you'll hear it this week. The antidote is to simply agree: "Yes, that is really impressive."

GAMES are win-lose transactions with a negative payoff, usually a **kick me**. Here are two:

1. You've had a bad day and you slam the door when you get home (nonverbal cold prickly stroke). Your spouse raises her/his voice from another room: "What the hell was that? (verbal cold prickly). Walking (angrily)

to your spouse and standing nose-to-nose staring coldly (more cold pricklies) you say: "It's me, that's what." With fire in her/his eyes, your spouse coldly says: "Like I said, what the hell is *that!*" Just reading the lines doesn't make much sense. It's a kick me game between two irate *Parents* trying to kick the *Child* in the other person. It's called **Uproar**. Men have an edge, with a deeper, louder voice. Those who are more intellectual play a variation called **Museum**. Instead of trading insults, they rely on memories of situations where one hurt the feelings of the other. Women have the edge. The antidote is to apologize as soon a possible, owning responsibility, thus sopping the game.

2. Some games are difficult to detect. You and your spouse bought an expensive one-of-a-kind carpet and the first day it was laid you tracked mud over it. There was no scene. You got an icy stare ad figured you got off easy. A week later, the President is driving by your home and has to go to the bathroom. The Secret Service asks if you would provide your home and you agree.

After the Chief answers nature's call, you offer a cup of coffee, and the President graciously accepts. The Prez says: "My, that's a very nice carpet." Spouse says: "Yes, it's one-of-a-kind and very expensive." Pres says: "I can see it's very special and would mean a lot to me if I had it." Spouse asks: "What would think of someone who tracked mud over it the first day it was installed?" Prez says: "Such a person would be thoughtless and stupid." Spouse then looks directly at (and though) you and asks: "Sweetheart, do you know anyone like that?" It's a kick me called **NIGYSOB**, for "now I've got you, you SOB." The antidote is to humbly apologize as soon as possible to prevent escalation before you get nuked.

A **RACKET** is a selective, specialized game or set of games. Only the Adult can "see" the **Parent** and **Child** and **Parent, Adult,** and **Child** of others.

There are two strong protections against being gamed:

1. Center, ground yourself in your **Adult**. That is the only part of you who can see the **Parent, Adult,** and **Child** in others

and is also in direct contact with your **Parent** and **Child**. This will help you establish **intimacy** with other **Adults**. **Intimacy** is a game-free relationship between two **Adults**.

2. Have a **contract partner** to help you identify and limit your own Game playing and detect and avoid games of others. Your partner "contracts" with you for your help and you reciprocate by helping her/him do the same, thus a contract.

FOUR BASIC LIFE POSITIONS

1. I'm OK, you're OK (the ideal)
2. I'm OK, you're not OK (blaming parent, not OK Kid)
3. I'm *not* OK, you're OK (not OK Kid)
4. I'm *not* OK, you're *not* OK (kicked Kid)

A **SCRIPT** or **LIFE SCRIPT** is a repeated life position, usually a lifelong behavior pattern.

GENDER DIFFERENCES

Research studies consistently show that in childhood boys are competitive, aggressive, constrictive, individualists who value freedom. Girls are enablers, more social and interdependent, more open and sharing. Boys are less emotive, more controlling, defensive, avoidant, goal-focused problem solvers. Girls are more emotive, open to share their concerns and feelings, listen more, and are more empathic.

Girls show a biobehavioral that is more tend-to-befriend than fight-or-flight (Taylor et al, 2000). Researcher Sandra Witelson found female brains "no better or worse" but there are "subtle differences" from birth. Neurons are "hard wired for outbound signals" 12% closer than in males in layers 2 and 4 which helps explain why tested IQ can be similar despite brain size and weight.

At USC Irvine, researchers found that even when tested IQ is similar, men and women use different parts of their brains to encode memory, sense emotion, recognize faces, solve problems, and make decisions, as if "from separate blueprints." Carl Jung described gender differences as *animus* (masculine) and *anima* (feminine) present in men and women. Sandra Bem suggested the goal be an enriching *androgyny* when man and women can function well together enjoying their differences.

EMERGING TRUTH: Men and women are "wired differently" so brain function differs but those differences attract more than repel and are challenges to transcend "masculinity" and "femininity" and value instead the uniqueness and charm of non-gender individual differences.

ASSERTIVENESS

You have an inherent right to ...
   ... be treated with dignity and respect
   ... say "No" without guilt
   ... take time to think
   ... ask questions
   ... express your opinion and feelings
   ... change your mind
   ... make mistakes
   ... feel good about yourself

To develop a positive attitude ...
... speak clearly and keep it simple
... use "I" language – own your thoughts
   and feelings
... agree to disagree and accept the views
   and feelings of others
... appreciate differences as well as
   similarities

SKILL BUILDERS

1. *Defense mechanisms.* Go over the list of *defense mechanisms.* Which do you use? Which do you use most? What does this tell you about yourself? What can you do to stop using them?

2. *Strokes!* Do you give *warm fuzzies?* Too many? Hardly any? *Cold pricklies? Plastic fuzzies?* Are you satisfied with the strokes you give? How can you improve using them?

3. *Discovering your Parent.* Think of + and – *Parent* behaviors of your real-life parents and grand-parents. How many do *you* have? Are they positive and appropriate? If not, work on replacing them with more appropriate behaviors to be a more of a
+ Parent!

4. *Meet your Child.* How's your *Child?* More OK than not? Recognize *Not OK Kid* feelings. When you have them find ways to offset them with an *OK Kid* mental hug ("you're still OK") or + Parent "pat on the back." Hurt feelings are inevitable but should not be taken as a judgment of your self-worth.

5. *Explore your Adult.* How active and effective is your *Adult*? Does it mediate well between your *Parent* and *Child*? If not, how can you improve it to make your *Parent, Adult,* and *Child* a happy family?

6. **Your PAC.** If your *Parent, Adult,* and *Child* were circles, would they be the same size? If not, what can you do to equalize them?

7. *Games.* What is the *PAC* interaction in sexual harassment? How much + and - *Parent, Adult,* and + and - *Child* of each person is involved? What should it be?

8. *Game prevention.* How can you be sure you *don't* play games? Who would be a good contract partner for you?

9. *Talk tactics.* Go over the talk tactics. Which do you use? Which *don't* you use? Try to develop skill in all of them so you can do what is most appropriate in every situation.

PARTING THOUGHT

I expect to pass through this world
but once; any good that I can do or
any kindness I can show, let me do it
now; let me not defer or neglect it,
for I shall not pass this way again.

-- Etienne de Grellet

3
WHAT THE HELL
ARE YOU DOING?
Problems, decisions,
coping with problem people

Take calculated risks.
That isn't the same as
being rash.
-- Gen. George S, Patton

REVISITING THE SCIENTIFIC METHOD

Here's the *scientific method* applied to problem solving and decision making:

1. Break the problem down into *workable parts*
2. *Brainstorm alternative solutions* and list advantages and disadvantages
3. Prepare a *backup plan* as an alternative and list its advantages and disadvantages
4. *Go for it! Do it!*
5. Use a *feedback loop* to evaluate progress and to *make any changes.*

SIMPLIFY -- BE A GOOD <u>KISSER</u>!

KISS is an acronym for *Keep It Simple, Sweetheart* (let's drop *Stupid* and choose to be positive!). **KISS** means avoiding double-talk, jargon, and technical language and, instead, use simple wording. Be a simplifier, not a complicater. Which are you? How good a **KISS**er are you? To find out, read this paragraph then summarize it *in one simple sentence.*

Human perceptual processing varies considerably both phylogenetically and idiosyncratically, subject to intrinsic and extrinsic variables. Genetic endowment and predisposition are intrinsic variables and situation-specific phenomena such as figure-ground, relative illumination, and operative distracting environmental cues are extrinsic variables. Either or both extrinsic and intrinsic factors obfuscate differential discrimination of visual stimuli. Ornithic behavior offers a heuristic example, where an avian species member of special interest eludes closer scrutiny and identification by classificatory schema. Experience confirms it is practicable to focus attention on one typical specimen tactually rather than by secondary visual attention of others of the same or similar species.

COPING WITH PROBLEM PEOPLE

HIDDEN AGENDAS

In her book *Peoplemaking,* Virginia Satir described five *hidden agendas* in people and organizations. Four are negative and one is positive.

1.   **BLAMING,** finding fault, disagreeing and being disagreeable, because you feel no one else makes any sense. Getting work done and reaching decisions really don't matter because it'll all be wrong anyway.

2. **PLACATING,** sweet talking, peace at any price, because you believe everyone should be nice and get along regardless of differences. That's more important than getting work done or reaching decisions.

3. **IRRELEVANT,** going off on tangents and avoiding getting to the point because you believe we never have enough detailed information. Data gathering is as important as deciding. The work can wait.

4. **SUPER REASONABLE,** is accepting everyone's opinion regardless of its value because everyone has a right to an opinion and there may be some great truth in whatever anyone says or does. Discussion is better than deciding.

5. **CONGRUENT,** is being "together," the ideal agenda, is being reasonable, honest, positive, and open, using facts and common sense, communicating clearly, and helping others express themselves.

DETECTING PROBLEM PEOPLE

Though their personality and specific behaviors vary, problem people share distinctive characteristics. The problem behavior is obvious to others as a negative repeated pattern of behavior. Coping is easier when you understand why and how they got that way. They all share one factor: *their behavior pays off,* usually a long-term or lifelong pattern from early childhood and reinforced for many years.

Because it is deeply rooted there is little or nothing you can do to change it. Besides, you don't have the time and you're not a mental health professional. Try to change them and you will have needless additional stress. It isn't worth it. *You* may even become a problem person yourself! Instead, learn to cope to minimize or prevent their behavior from interfering with you and others. Be positive. Consider them an opportunity to deepen your understanding and improve coping skills. The greater their problem behavior, the more you can grow coping with them.

1. BULLDOZER, usually male with "a short fuse," bully or barking dog.

Their strategy: Overpower, might makes right, nice guys finish last. Over-reacting keeps everybody away at a safe distance. Bosses back down.

Their tactics: Shoot first, think later; blast, over-react, outshout others.

Effect on others: Fear, avoidance.

Recommended coping: Don't fight. You'll lose! Try a 1-2-3 takedown: "I hear you (1) but I wonder if … (2) … and what others think" and (3) sidestep their anger, let them bark (vent) within reason.

2. BADMOUTH, a chronic complainer, critic, and griper, usually with an acid tongue.

Their strategy: Finding fault is the best way to win and feel good about yourself and prove your self-worth.

Their tactics: Always criticize, belittle, put down anyone and anything.

Effect on others: Disillusionment, avoidance, a major negative influence.

Recommended coping: Be positive. Calmly, confidently continue. Don't get hooked emotionally.

3. LOST SOUL, a clinging vine, wet blanket, drifting helplessly.

Their strategy: The world is a dangerous place and I can't make it!

Their tactics: Be helpless and there will always be someone to rescue you.

Effect on others: Frustration, irritation, anger, avoidance.

Recommended coping: Don't be a rescuer! Continual rescues can lower standards, erode team spirit, and keep lost souls passive. Encourage involvement and compliment them whenever they take the initiative -- emphasize *they* did it, a personal achievement.

4. SWEETHEART, sickeningly sweet, super agreeable but superficial.

Their strategy: Be nice and everyone will be nice to you. No need to do anything, just smile and be sweet and everyone will love you.

Their tactics: Do little or nothing, keep smiling, and never criticize.

Effect on others: Avoidance, distrust, impatience

Recommended coping: Reward them for being critical. Reparenting them or being *their* sweetheart just makes them more passive.

5. SANDBAGGER is a foot dragger, procrastinator, passive obstructionist.

Their strategy: Delay long enough and you win. Change is bad anyway. Anything new is dangerous: "If it ain't broke, don't fix it."

Their tactics: Use every possible roadblock to avoid work and change.

Effect on others: Avoidance. Their negativism is contagious.

Recommended coping: Try to match every negative with a positive. Calmly state or repeat goals and what's needed. Be patient, steadfast. Keep cool. Seeing you sweat encourages them.

6. EXPERT is really an expert who is knowledgeable, skilled, experienced, tends to overthink and obsess, often with less common sense.

Their strategy: Knowledge is power. Not knowing is failure.

Their tactics: Consciously or unintentionally put down others.

Effect on others: Inferiority feeling, avoidance, lowered morale.

Recommended coping: Acknowledge, accept, and use their expertise, but if necessary take the ball back with: "Yes, and it may also be that …"

7. THE ECCENTRIC is a loner with unusual thinking or eccentric behavior, usually socially withdrawn.

Their strategy: Don't grow up. Being a kid with childish fantasy or being different is safer and better.

Their tactics: They behave as if they are in a
world to themselves, daydream, are easily
distracted, and have difficulty following
direction.

Effect on others: Avoidance

Recommended coping: Involve them. Help
them keep focused.

8. SECRET AGENT, the most dangerous,
usually above average intelligence but
devious, deceptive, and conspiring.

Their strategy: The sweetest victory is
winning by clever manipulation and
outsmarting authority figures they see as
stupid and deserve to lose anyway.

Their tactics: Subtly, indirectly, covertly
outwit and outmaneuver everyone,
especially authority figures. The end
always justifies the means. Deceive and
involve others to help.

Effect on others: Avoidance, fear, and feeling
used and dirty.

Recommended coping: Avoid 1-to-1 conversation (can later be denied, distorted, or
to start a rumor. Keep contact public,
witnessed. Be aware they usually recruit
followers unaware of their real intent.

DO'S AND DON'TS

1. **DO** keep a safe, optimal distance without isolating yourself from them. You need to keep them in sight.
2. **DO** focus on work to be done, not personal differences.
3. **DO** shift into the scientific method of problem solving.
4. **DO** stay focused, centered, grounded. Do not get distracted.
5. **DON'T** get emotionally involved. That's how they win.
6. **DON'T** try to change them -- it's a lifelong pattern.
7. **DON'T** fight. That it takes time, energy, and stress and you may well lose.
8. **DON'T** ignore them. Focus on neutralizing their effect (damage control).
9. **DON'T** play games. They're better at it. If in a game, center in your *Adult* and either call the game or decline to play.

FIVE NEVERS

1. **NEVER** put down or belittle anyone,

   except yourself which is always OK.
2. **NEVER** lecture. It can sound

   condescending like a – *Parent.*
3. **NEVER** raise your voice or order people

   around. It looks like you're losing it.
4. **NEVER** threaten, ridicule, harass or probe

   needlessly.
5. **NEVER** lose control. If you're getting

   upset, take a break.

COPING TACTICS

1. STAY COOL!

Ground, center, stabilize yourself physically and mentally. If seated, sit upright, solidly balanced on the chair, both feet on the floor. Be aware of your breathing. Keep it regular. There's a tendency to breathe more rapidly when stressed and that can lead to more anxiety. A good way to take time to relax more and cope better is by first *thanking them*: "I want to thank you for sharing your (suggestion, thoughts, feelings). I appreciate that." As we were taught in childhood "please" and "thank you" are *magic words*. They can disarm, defuse, and cool heated situations.

2. APOLOGIZE even if you're right!

It's *word magic*. "I can see you're upset and I'm sorry about that," then acknowledge *your* feelings: "It's upsetting for me, too." Expressing regret does not mean conceding anything. This does not weaken but actually strengthens your position, shows your openness, and can pay off if the matter goes to a higher level. Many lawsuits are by people who feel wronged and would not have sued if there had been a simple apology earlier.

3. STATE YOUR CASE calmly and clearly.

Stick to facts not feelings. Try *reframing* the situation by referring to "it," not you or the problem person. Then, if conflict continues the conversation can be more objective, less personal. It is easier to negotiate or resolve a situation when both parties stick to facts and avoid personalities. Many problems are solved at this step.

4. MAKE AN OFFER

Try for a win-win exchange of gifts, what you consider a fair resolution. Try: "What can *we* do to correct it?" or "if you see a way to fairly solve this I'll gladly work with you on it." At this stage you can shift into the steps of the scientific method.

5. SIDESTEP CHARGING BULLS.

Be a matador. Ignore irrelevant behavior. "Be kind to dumb animals." Some leaders overreact, overdo, and overkill. *Choose* not to be the victim. Insulate, isolate, ground and center yourself.

6. DISARM – GRACIOUSLY

"I appreciate your input...I'm always willing to listen...sorry if what I said offended you...I hear what you're saying but..." Express your openness, then what's needed. It encourages others to do the same.

7. COLUMBO TACTIC

Adapt and lower yourself, put yourself down by playing dumb: "I get confused sometimes, so let me see if I understand this correctly, if we ___, then ___ is likely to happen. Do you agree?" Often the other person provides loopholes not obvious before when the problem situation is repeated.

8. HUMOR

Humor can be an effective coolant and lubricant to overheated verbal engines but to do so it must be used wisely and well. It should never be used if there's any chance it can be misconstrued or to attack or hurt. To develop this skill watch TV comedies, read comic strips, and observe humorous situations in everyday life.

9. VELVET GLOVE or SCREWDRIVER

This is a soft sell indirect approach that usually begins with "I wonder if we could ___" or "could it be that ___ ?"

10. SANDWICHING, PAIRING

Sandwiching is enclosing a negative comment between positive statements. For example: "That's pretty good, but you might try ___ which be even better." *Pairing* is matching a negative with a positive comment, thus softening the blow but still delivering a corrective message: "That's not our usual style, probably a minor glitch."

11. DO NOTHING -- WELL!

In ancient China, Laotse knew about confused situations. He compared them to muddy water. Left alone, undisturbed, it usually clears by itself. Some conflict situations fade over time. It's also true that "mighty oaks from tiny acorns grow" and it may be wiser to resolve conflicts when they are small and prevent them from getting worse. It's a judgment call and test of leadership skill.

TALK TACTICS TOOLBOX

1. SILENCE is one of the most effective and *least used* verbal tactics. It is the *strategic* use of pauses, pacing, time, and timing. Common *misuse* is to wait too long to say something or, conversely, to speak too quickly or interrupt a "heavy" conversation breaking the mood.

2. SUPPORT, given to reassure, sympathize with, or encourage verbally or nonverbally with a nod, wink, pat, or gesture.

3. SELF-DISCLOSURE is sharing your own personal experiences in past or present similar situations. Use it wisely! Confessing too much weakness might lessen confidence in your leadership ability or competence.

4. INDIRECT APPROACH. This is the "velvet glove" approach of subtly leading the conversation by asking questions such as "What else could you/we do? ... I wonder if ... what would happen if ... or the *Columbo technique*: "I don't know, I'm not too sure, but maybe you could ..."

5. DIRECT CONFRONTATION. This can be *tough love* or a softer *telling it like it is*. Use when there is little time for discussion or a firm decision must be made but use it cautiously at other times because of possible negative effect.

6. ASK QUESTIONS. This is the "Socratic method" encourages more or deeper thought, reflection, reframing. Don't overdo it. That might seem badgering or belittling.

7. HELP EXPLORE ALTERNATIVES, best done *indirectly* or it may sound like you're being domineering.

8. CLARIFY. Stop and review, rephrase, reframe the situation. This cools hot topics, allows more time to vent hurt feelings, go to better closure.

9. HERE AND NOW FOCUS, limited to what's happening at the moment with no reference to the past.

10. THERE AND THEN FOCUS, digging deeper into the past for what's behind or beneath present problem.

11. PHYSICAL FOCUS on facial expression, posture, and mannerisms: "I can see you're upset and I want to do whatever I can to help..."

12. VERBAL BEHAVIOR FOCUS on what is said, and how (tone of voice, rate of speech, choice of words). "I hear you and I want to help..."

13. FEELINGS FOCUS on what you or the other person is feeling rather than the facts involved: "How do you feel about it?" A useful question! You may not agree with a person's feelings but allowing those feelings to be vented relieves tension, often for both of you.

14. HUMOR can be an effective icebreaker, to lessen distance, lower resistance and defenses, and cool hot tempers. Time, timing, and content are important. Never use it to ridicule or laugh at anyone, except yourself which is always OK. To be effective, humor must be natural and not forced or hostile.

WHAT'S NORMAL?

"What's normal?" is a simple question not so easily answered. *Human behavior is complex and multicausational.* Dictionaries offer several definitions, from "according with, constituting, or not deviating from a norm, rule, or principle" to "conforming to a type, standard, or regular pattern" to "from mental disorder." What's normal is more a matter of degree than kind. Most people have tendencies toward something abnormal but do not act on them.

In one sense, "normal" is *whatever society says it is.* Nude family bathing is normal in Japan but not in he U.S. Russian generals kiss soldiers on the mouth when pinning a medal on them. In France, kissing on both cheeks is the norm. What's normal can differ in *families*, such as the way they show affection, some more direct and physical than others. What's normal can involve **custom and tradition** and **religious belief,** such as forbidding drinking, games of chance, dancing, or certain foods.

What's normal can be a matter of **legal definition**. A 'keep off the grass" considers walking on the grass as violating a norm. Insanity, the most abnormal behavior, is specified by law. The psychiatric definition of what's abnormal is listed in the diagnostic manual (DSM) and psychologists define it as how behavior deviates from statistical norms. If "everybody's doing it" it's "normal."

What's normal can also be "in the eye of the beholder," such as someone who behaves in ways that differ from your own, what you see as odd or eccentric – abnormal. What's abnormal is listed in the bulky manual called "the DSM" (*Diagnostic and Statistical Manual of Mental Disorders*) of the American Psychiatric Association. It is based on a five-axial system to diagnose mental disorders. Using a checklist format, a list of symptoms that describe disorders. Axis I is the clinical diagnosis;   Axis II lists mental retardation or personality disorder); Axis III is any medical condition); Axis IV lists psychosocial factors; and Axis V is global function as a percentile. Here are the DSM mental disorders:

Mental disorders of infancy and childhood are diagnosed separately. They are: **mental retardation** (*mild, moderate, severe, or profound*); **learning disorder** (problem with a school subject in an otherwise normal child); **motor skills disorder; communication disorder** (speech problem); **pervasive developmental disorder** (*autism, Asperger's, Rett's, or disintegrative*); **attention-deficit** or **disruptive behavior** (*attention-deficit hyperactivity disorder, oppositional defiant or conduct disorder*; **feeding or eating disorder** (*pica,* eating non-food substances; *rumination, feeding disorder*; **tic disorder** (twitching, shouting); **elimination disorder:** *encopresis* (soiling); *enuresis* (bedwetting). Others: *separation anxiety; selective mutism; reactive adjustment disorder; stereotypic movement disorder.*

MENTAL DISORDERS
OF ADULTHOOD

COGNITIVE DISORDER

Dementia: *Alzheimer's* (most common, early or late, with or without disturbed behavior or delusions); **vascular dementia** with or without delusions or depression.

Delirium from *substance, medical condition, withdrawal,* or *multiple causes.*

DISSOCIATIVE DISORDERS

Amnesia; fugue; identity disorder (formerly multiple personality); **depersonalization disorder.**

EATING DISORDERS

Anorexia nervosa (self starvation); **bulimia nervosa** (binge-purge eating, often with diuretic or laxative abuse); **pica** (eating non-food substances).

SOMATOFORM DISORDERS

Conversion, somatization, pain disorders; hypochondria; body dysmorphia (body image disorder).

SCHIZOPHRENIA AND OTHER PSYCHOTIC DISORDERS

Brief psychotic disorder; shared psychotic disorder, delusional disorder (*erotomania, jealous, somatic, grandiose, or persecutory*); **schizophrenia**, first reported by Emil Kraepelin as *dementia praecox (paranoid, catatonic, disorganized, undifferentiated, or residual)*.

SLEEP DISORDERS

Dyssomnia: *insomnia, hypersomnia, apnea circadian rhythm* (sleep-wake cycle disorder), *narcolepsy* (sleep attacks at any time); **parasomnia:** *nightmare, sleepwalking, or sleep terror.*

FACTITIOUS DISORDER

Feigned sick role, can be *mainly psychological or physical, mixed,* or *by proxy* (induced by someone or something else).

MOOD/AFFECTIVE DISORDERS

Major depression, recurrent or single episode; **dysthymic disorder** (less severe); **bipolar affective disorder** (depressed or manic); **cyclothymic disorder** (less severe mood swings than bipolar disorder).

ANXIETY DISORDERS
Generalized, panic, specific phobia, social phobia, agoraphobia, acute stress, post-traumatic stress disorder (PTSD), or obsessive- compulsive disorder.

ADJUSTMENT DISORDERS
... with anxiety, depression, or mixed or with disturbed conduct or emotion or mixed.

IMPULSE CONTROL DISORDER
Kleptomania, pyromania, pathological gambling, intermittent explosive disorder, trichotillomania

SUBSTANCE ABUSE DISORDER
Abuse (occasional use) or **dependence** (addiction) to *alcohol, amphetamine, caffeine, cannabis, cocaine, hallucinogen, inhalant, nicotine, opioid, phencyclidine (PCP), anxiolytic, sedative, hypnotic,* or *polysubstance* (several substances).

SEXUAL OR GENDER IDENTITY
Sexual dysfunction (*of desire or arousal, an-orgasmic, or pain*); **paraphilias** (*exhibitionist, voyeur, fetishist, frotteur, pedophile, sadist, masochist, transvestic fetishist, gender identity disorder* (seeks sex change surgery).

PERSONALITY DISORDER
Paranoid, schizoid, schizotypal, antisocial, borderline, histrionic, narcissistic, avoidant, dependent, or **obsessive-compulsive** (long-term usually lifelong pattern with distinctive features that interfere with an otherwise normal lifestyle.

OTHER FACTORS (V codes)
Borderline intelligence, malingering, phase of life, identity, bereavement, accultu-ration, academic, occupational, spiritual-religious factors.

SKILL BUILDERS

1. *Revisiting the scientific method.* How can you apply the scientific method to buying a car? Clothing? Food?

2. *Learning to simplify.* Read one editorial a day and summarize its major premise. Imagine an opposing opinion. Do the same once a day watching TV news or an interview. What is most true, or is there a third position closer to the truth?

3. *Coping with difficult people.* Review the types of difficult people. Which type bothers you most? Study their strategies, tactics, and the best way to cope with them. Imagine the worst possible situation and mentally rehearse how you can handle it.

4. *Talk tactics.* How many of the *talk tactics* on page 5 do you use regularly? Which don't you use? Why not develop skill in all of them so you can freely choose which is most appropriate?

5. *What's abnormal?* Many movies portray abnormal behavior and classic therapies, such as *Fatal attraction* (paranoid eroto-mania), *Three faces of Eve* and *Sybil* (identity disorder), Freud and *Spellbound* (psycho-analysis), *Lovesick* (hilarious parody of Freudian theory), *One flew over the cuckoo's* *nest* and *Frances* (therapies in the 1940s and 1950s). While some movies are "Holly-woodized," they are a good way to observe disturbed behavior.

PARTING THOUGHTS

The world is moving so fast, the
person who says it can't be done
is interrupted by someone doing it
-- Elbert Hubbard

Do all the good you can, by all the means you can, in all the ways you can, in all the places you can, at all the times you can, to all the people you can, as long as ever you can.

-- John Wesley

4
WELLNESS
Counseling skills;
fighting burnout

> Love your enemies.–
> It'll drive'em crazy!
> -- saying

The behavioral sciences have many examples of a normal, healthy personality and behavior. The treatment methods used to provide therapy is another useful source of information, such as:

PSYCHOANALYTIC-PSYCHODYNAMIC THERAPY is *historical* (going back to sources), then *processing* early sources of problems. The goal is to strengthen the ego to overcome the id (primitive self, instinctive drives) and mediate the superego (conscience). As Freud put it, "where id is, ego shall be." He saw this as freeing the self of wasted energy such as in defense mechanisms, and watch "as repression passes in review."

BEHAVIORIST THERAPIES such as cognitive, dialectic behavior, rational-emotive, rational living, reality therapies are based on the *cognitive model*, that thoughts cause feelings and behavior, not external factors. Albert Elis founded rational-emotive therapy, one of the older behaviorist methods that helps overcome false beliefs and their effects. He said we should be aware of these unhealthy "ABC's"

A = Activating event/situation

B = Belief

C = Consequence(s) (upset feelings)

And, Ellis said we should add D and E:

D = Dispute them -- question/critique them)

E = Effect a better effect, what you prefer to have happen.

COGNITIVE-BEHAVIORALTHERAPY or **(CBT)** blends cognitive and behaviorist therapies which co-existed as separate therapies but are effective when combined. The major premise is that most emotional and behavioral reactions are learned and can therefore be unlearned. CBT therapists listen for what you want then help you achieve it. It focuses on benefits of remaining calm in stressful situations. When upset there are two problems: *it* and *getting upset.* You can be upset in situations that really aren't what you *think* they are. CBT teaches you to ask questions like: "How do I know people are laughing at me? Could they be laughing about something else?" It is fact-based, not on assumptions or fears, and develops non-judgmental thinking, seeing thoughts as **unproven possibilities to be tested.**

SYSTEMATIC DESENSITIZATION is a treatment to gradually replace a learned fear or anxiety with a relaxed response and greater self-control. There are three basic steps: first, compiling a list of anxiety-producing situations, in rank order; second, learning how to use visual imagery and muscle relaxation; and third, pairing the imagery and relaxation with anxiety-producing thoughts, feelings, and situations.

SOLUTION-ORIENTED BRIEF THERAPY is another trend in therapy that is cognitive-behavioral. Its basic principles:

1. **CHANGE IS CONSTANT**. You're body is not the same as it was yesterday and neither is your mind.

2. **CHANGE IS CONTAGIOUS**. Change little things and big ones are easier to manage and change.

3 **NOTHING IS EVER HOPELESS**. Many others have had the same problem and overcame it.

4. **YOU MAY ALREADY HAVE THE ANSWER!** Listen to your "Eternal Child." Many times the best solution is the simplest.

5. **MIRACLE QUESTION.** If you woke up tomorrow and the problem bothering you miraculously disappeared, how would you know it? What would be the first sign? How would things be different? Who would notice? What would *you* be like? Bottom line: How can you be like that *right now?*

6. **ACCENTUATE THE POSITIVE.** Negativism can be neutralized by

emphasizing *anything* positive. Look closer. Find something positive. If you do something well, ask yourself how you did it. Next time, do that again. Give yourself a mental pat on the back when you do something well, especially a disagreeable task. When you feel down, remember positive accomplishments. Make a list of ways to apply positive thinking, then do it.

7. **MENTAL REHEARSAL**. Doing "pretend problems" and how you'd solve them helps you prepare for the real thing.

8. **DON'T OVER-WORRY**. Mark Twain said: "I've lived a long time and most of what I worried about never happened." Schedule and limit worry times to five to 10 minutes a day.

9. **DON'T LABEL OR USE STEREOTYPES**. Give people a chance to be themselves. You may be pleasantly surprised.

10. **AVOID SELF-FULFILLING PROPHECIES**. They encourage negativism and invite disaster.

11. **FORGET PAST NEGATIVES** (after you've processed them) as lessons of what not to do next time. You've probably put yourself down enough about them. As poet Carl Sandburg wrote: "The past is a bucket of dead ashes."

12. **USE FAILURE** as an opportunity to put a positive spin on it.

13. **MAKE A STRENGTHS LIST** of past "goods" and refer to it to maintain a positive attitude and when you need a boost of self-esteem.

14. **BUILD ON POSITIVE EXCEPTIONS** and magnify them! There's a ripple effect like dropping a pebble in a still pond.

15. Develop and use your **SENSE OF HUMOR**. Yes, you *do* have one. Watch TV comedies, newspaper and magazine cartoons and read the comic strips.
16. **BE PATIENT!** Rome wasn't built in a day. Neither is changing an attitude. 2500 years in ancient China, the poet-philosopher LaoTse wrote: "A journey of 1000 miles begins with the first step."

THE THREE E's

Ferdinand ("Fritz") Perls, founder of gestalt therapy, suggested everyone follow *the three E's: be here now* (**E**xistential), *be real"*(**E**xperiential), *take risks* (**E**xperimental).

FIGHT BURNOUT!

BURNOUT is *physical and/or emotional exhaustion from continued unvented stress.* The antidote is to **fight it**. If you don't, it's like swimming in an alligator infested swamp. Eventually, you're gonna get bitten! Some stress is unavoidable and can be a good tonic for mind and body. George Bernard Shaw said: "I'd rather wear out than rust out." If stress continues or increases without being vented or neutralized, burnout increases and can lead to serious medical or mental problems.

SIGNS OF BURNOUT

PHYSICAL: fatigue, disturbed sleep, increased or decreased appetite, startle response (being jumpy), and psychosomatic disorders.

EMOTIONAL: irritability, mood swings, anxiety and/or depression, feeling helpless, disillusioned, or discouraged.

PSYCHOLOGICAL: personality or behavior change, depersonalization ("I'm not myself...this is not me" or others tell you "you don't seem to be yourself"), derealization ("This isn't happening...it's unreal"), or social withdrawal.

SPIRITUAL: feelings of meaninglessness, emptiness, fatalistic attitude.

GENERAL ADAPTATION SYNDROME (GAS)

Canadian psychologist Hans Selye spent decades researching animals and humans under stress. In his book *The stress of life,* he described a 3-phase burnout process he called the *General Adaptation Syndrome* or GAS. He found that regardless of the type of stress, response to it goes through three stages:

1. **ALARM,** the arousal phase. Heart and breathing rate increase and anxiety level is higher than usual. You *feel* stressed.
2. **RESISTANCE.** Anxiety seems to decrease because the body has adjusted to it, but there are often unnoticed changes in body chemistry and the immune system weakens, lowering resistance to disease.
3. **EXHAUSTION,** the final most dangerous phase. Body chemistry and organ systems reach life-threatening potential and can result in death!

OTHER ASPECTS

In their book *Burnout,* Edelwich and Brodsky described a 4-stage process, each stage, like a fork in the road where you decide which way to go. This is not a conscious process when circumstances or situations move you to one side or the other:

Enthusiasm or **realism** then to

Activity or **stagnation** then to

Satisfaction or **frustration** then to

Involvement or **apathy**

In their article *Characteristics of burnout,* Pines and Maslach described burnout as levels in a downward spiral:

Emotional exhaustion leads to

Cynicism and insensitivity

and that leads to

Low self concept *("I'm a total failure")*

SUGGESTIONS

1. **RECOGNIZE AND ACCEPT LIMITS.**

   Do the best you can, then let go.

2. **PRIORITIZE.** Change the order of things

   to avoid boredom. Keeps you fresh.

3. **BITE THE BULLET.** Don't put off

   disagreeable tasks.

4. **CHOOSE TO BE POSITIVE** in any negative situation.

5. **TOLERATE AND FORGIVE.** Don't carry extra baggage. It clutters the mind.

6. Use stressful situations to **INOCULATE** you against future stress.

7. **VENT APPROPRIATELY** (jog, garden, putter, listen to music, get a hobby).

8. **LEARN TO RELAX MORE,** to let go, in that childlike, dog/cat-nap space.

9. **HAVE FUN.** Laugh more. Find or do something funny every day.

10. **TAKE CARE OF YOURSELF.** Exercise, eat sensibly, have regular medical checkups, don't smoke, drink in moderation.

MINISCRIPTS

Everyone has a *miniscript* according to therapist Taibi Kahler. It's like an audiotape that plays automatically in your head with a judgmental blaming message the instant something goes wrong. Kahler estimated that by age five you've heard 25,000 hours of these messages from your parents. They are summarized as five *miniscript <u>drivers</u>:*

> I **must** *try harder*
>
> I **must** *be perfect*
>
> I **must** *be strong*
>
> I **must** *hurry*
>
> I **must** *please him/her/them/me*

If not neutralized, *drivers* are magnified into *stoppers*:

> **I failed again!**
>
> **I could (or should) have done better!**
>
> **I really let him/her/them/ms down!**

The resulting feeling: *I'm not OK but you're OK*. If not neutralized, *stoppers* move to the mental dead end of *Final Miniscript Position (FMP)* of *I'm not OK, you're not OK, nothing's OK.* This can result in alcohol or drug abuse, divorce, getting fired, even suicide. The best way to prevent this downward spiral is to *neutralize a driver the instant it hooks you* with a memorized, automatic *allower* specific to the driver that started it all:

It's OK to sometimes make a mistake

It's OK to do and not overdo

It's OK to take care of *myself*!

It's OK to be me (or write your own!)

Most people hear one or two *drivers* more than others. *Memorize* **the** *allower* for it so you will hear it the instant the *driver* is heard. It helps to post allowers where you can easily see them such as at the phone, on your desk or refrigerator.

THE PURSUIT OF HAPPINESS

It's interesting to note that the *Declaration of Independence* guarantees every citizen the right to life, liberty, and the *pursuit* of happiness. It doesn't guarantee happiness, just pursuing it. It shows wise insight because only you can know (or should know) what it takes to make you happy. Therapist Carl Rogers considered *unrealistic expectations* the root cause of unhappiness.

The "Hollywood version" of happiness is Snow White waiting for Prince Charming to carry her off on a white horse to his castle to live "happily ever after." It's an unrealistic expectation. Happiness as a goal of and by itself leads to disillusionment and even depression, the direct opposite of happiness.

Happiness is more a by-product than the product, a direction not a destination. Therapist Psychologist Gordon Allport said "happiness is not itself a motivating force but a by-product of otherwise motivated activity." Humorist Josh Billings wrote: "If you ever find happiness by hunting for it you will find it, like the old lady found her lost spectacles, safe on her nose all the time." And actor John Barrymore said "happiness sneaks in through a door you didn't know you left open."

Wilfred Peterson wrote that "happiness is found in little things: a baby's smile, a letter from a friend, the song of a bird, a light in the window." You can see happiness in others, such as a child with a new puppy or long-awaited birthday or Christmas present, the eyes of lovers, a returning veteran from war. In *The art of living,*

There are three levels of happiness: adjustment, contentment, joy. Adjustment, openly accepting yourself and your life situation and "making peace" with both. That leads to contentment, happy with who you are and what you have. Charles Haddon Spurgeon wrote "it's not how much we have but how much we enjoy what we have that makes happiness."

Joy is the peak of happiness, and happens spontaneously, serendipitously, like children at play, at the circus, or you at Mardi Gras or a party. Poet Carl Sandburg warned against getting carried away or obsessed with being happy:

> Are you happy? It's the only way to
>   be, kid.
> Yes, be happy, it's a good nice way
>   to be.
> But not happy-happy, kid.
> Don't be too doubled-up doggone
>   happy.
> It's the doubled up doggone happy-
>   happy people who bust hard.
> They do bust hard when they bust.
> Be happy, kid, go for it, bit not too
>   doggone happy.

Happiness can come interacting with people. In her poem *Little Things*, Julia

Fletcher put it simply: "Little deeds of kindness, little words of love, help to make earth happy, like the heaven above." In *The art of living*, Wilfred Peterson wrote: "You can't pursue happiness and catch it. Happiness comes upon you unawares while you are helping others, like the old Hindu proverb: 'Help your brother's boat across and lo, your own has reached the shore."

And in *IF and AND*, W.P. King wrote: "If you can think about your work as helping someone else you will soon find that alone makes your task happier. And if you add to each task some little touch that goes beyond what is required, your work becomes a thing of art and leads to a realm where pleasure lives and drudgery dies. And this domain of artistry has ample room for hope and dreams and spreading wings and little songs to make the day eternal dawn.

There is happiness communing with nature, as Lizette Woodworh Reese found:

Glad that I live am I, that the sky is
   blue;
Glad for the country lanes and the
   fall of snow.

After the sun the rain, after the rain
   the sun;
That is the way of life, till the work
   be done.
All that we need to do, be we low or
   high,
Is to see that we grow nearer the sky

So, what can you do to be happier? Most experts suggest not actively searching for it, but enjoying every moment we find it. Charles Schulz, creator of the popular *Peanuts* cartoon series, described happiness as "a thumb and a blanket, a pile of leaves to jump into, a warm puppy, finding someone you like at the front door, friends in a sandbox with no fighting, roller skating on a smooth sidewalk, climbing a tree, after hiccups go away, walking in grass with bare feet, a box of crayons with 18 colors." A

Happiness is a "to each her/his own" individual experience. It's "whatever turns your crank," aptly described by Gwendolen Haste in *Montana wives* (1930):
   I had to laugh.
   When she said it, we were sitting
by the door, and straight down was

the fork, twisting and turning and gleaming in the sun, and your eyes carried beyond the river with the Beartooth Mountain fairly screaming with light and blue and snow, and fold and turn of rimrock, and prairies as far as your eye could go.

And she said: "Dear Laura, sometimes I feel so sorry for you, shut away from everything, eating out your heart with loneliness. When I think of my own full life I wish I could share it with you. Just pray for happier days, and bear it."

She went back to Billings to her white stucco house, and a brick house, and a yellow frame house, and six trimmed poplar trees, and little squares of shaved grass.

Oh dear. She stared at me like I was daft. I couldn't help it. I just laughed and laughed.

EXERCISE. This is an important exercise! What are you now aware of from happiness from reading the above material? What can you do to enjoy life more, to be happier? Do it!

WELLNESS

To fight burnout effectively you need to be relatively happy and in good physical and mental health. Here are 15 ways to be and stay well:

1. **BE YOURSELF AND GET EXCITED ABOUT IT!** Accept yourself. be the best you can be. Ralph Waldo Emerson said: "Make the most of yourself. That's all there is of you."

2. **RECOGNIZE AND ACCEPT LIMITS.** Do all you can and when you can do no more, *let go of it!*

3. **PRIORITIZE.** Re-arrange your schedule to keep fresh. Change the order of things to avoid boredom. Try doing disagreeable tasks first, while you're fresh.

4. **SCHEDULE WORRY TIMES,** such as 5 to 10 minutes a day and no more. Worry can wear you down. If you get a bill there is no deduction for worrying about it.

5. **BE POSITIVE.** Consciously, deliberately, *choose* to be positive. Find something positive in a negative situation. End the day remembering and reflecting on one positive thing that happened.

6. **TOLERATE AND FORGIVE.** Don't carry any extra baggage (unfinished mental business). It clutters the mind.

7. **BE A MATADOR.** Sidestep the charging bull of someone's anger or frustration. Choose not to be the target. *It* is the problem (or *he* or *she) –the bull* -- not you. Don't choose to be the target.

8. **USE STRESS AS AN INOCULATION,** to learn from it and use it to improve coping skills. You will grow stronger, not weaker, from every setback.

9. **VENT.** Learn ways to "get it out of your system" with a contract partner, by gardening, washing the car, jogging, walking, listening to relaxing music, etc. It is helpful to have a contract partner you *contract* with to share personal thoughts and feelings. It's a contract because both of you agree to join in a special kind of dialog.

10. **TAKE CARE OF YOUR BODY** with exercise, good nutrition, and regular medical checkups. Try eating slower, and a bit less. And, stop smoking!

11. **TAKE TIME OUTS**, mini-vacations, fun breaks. You need and them and you deserve them! Examples: Go "away" in a garden, church or temple, library (just sit!), park bench, or comfy chair.

12. **LEARN TO DO NOTHING -- WELL.** Relax *totally* in that restful, childlike, dog or cat-nap OK feeling. Experience it more often.

13. **LAUGH MORE.** Notice something funny every day. If you can't find anything funny, do something silly yourself! Read the comics, watch comedy movies, and share in jokes.

14. **BE A KID MORE.** Hug the *Eternal Child* inside you. When's the last time you had an ice cream cone? Chewed bubble gum – and popped it?

15. **GET A HOBBY**, one more physical than mental, more restful than tedious.

MINDFULNESS

Guided imagery is a self-relaxation technique to neutralize stress. Visualize a relaxing imaginary place you can go to escape from stress. Many choose a sandy ocean beach, others a beautiful garden or forest. Avoid imagining a real place. That can bring memories that interfere. You must be alone. If others are there it becomes social interaction. If strolling on a beach is relaxing, imagine it *in slow motion.* Jogging or walking are not as deeply relaxing.

If other thoughts interrupt, *don't fight them.* That takes energy. Instead, focus on *details* of your peaceful place such as sand, grass, flowers, trees, birds, sky, clouds, a soft breeze, scent of flowers or pine needles, etc. Treat invading thoughts like a TV commercial you see but don't attend to. They will fade as you focus on details of your peaceful place and gain more experience going there.

Every day take a moment to imagine being in your peaceful place. Opportune times are on a break, a moment after breakfast, at your desk, waiting for someone, relaxing in a chair, even on the toilet. Take a deep breath and go there to strengthen the relaxing effect. In time, it will happen automatically. You'll take a deep breath while visualizing your peaceful place whenever you begin to feel stress. You'll know it's working as your body relaxes.

Imagine yourself in your peaceful place every night as you fall asleep. In a comfortable position, eyes closed, take one or two long, slow deep breaths, and then breathe normally as you fall asleep. If you awaken during the night, return to sleep visualizing your peaceful place. *Be there.* To further develop this technique, once a day lie in a restful position on your back, legs slightly parted, head on a pillow or use a recliner chair. A 30-minute cassette recorder that clicks off at tape end provides 15 minutes on one side. Record and play soft music at low volume or "white sound" like ocean surf from static on a blank radio or TV channel, for the 15 minutes. Some use a blank tape that clicks off at 15 minutes. Use whatever works best for you.

If other thoughts interrupt *don't fight them.* That takes energy. Instead, focus on *details* of your peaceful place such as sand, grass, flowers, trees, birds, sky, clouds, a soft breeze, scent of flowers or pine needles, etc. Treat invading thoughts like a TV commercial you see but don't attend to. They will fade as you focus on details of your peaceful place and gain more experience going there.

When stressed, be aware of your breathing. Keep it regular, not hurried. Anxiety can cause faster breathing and breathing normally helps prevent it. Annoying interruptions can be deactivated by pairing them with relaxing details of your peaceful place. On a bad day, take a short break alone in a quiet place, sit, eyes closed, take a deep breath and for a minute or two relax in your peaceful place. Guided imagery can be a non-drug tranquilizer!

DEVELOP AN EARLY WARNING SYSTEM

Another way to minimize the negative effect of stress is to develop your own *early warning system* at the first sign of stress. What happens to you when you are stressed? What's the first sign? Everyone has a weak spot where anxiety is first felt.

For some it's a dry mouth, for others a change in voice, throbbing head, rapid heart rate, fast breathing, butterflies in the stomach, or nervous twitch. Be instantly aware of your body's first sign of stress -- your early warning system. As soon as you feel it, imagine your peaceful place, take a break, switch and do something else, or change your routine. Doing nothing allows stress to build.

PREVENTING SUICIDE

In most years, 30,000 people commit suicide. That's about 85 a day. Another 500,000 try it but don't succeed. The rate for teenagers has quadrupled over the past 20 years, It and has doubled for children under 14. There are more suicides and attempts than reported. Many accidental deaths are suicides. Freud called suicide "murder in the 180th degree," anger or rage turned inward and at one's self. Suicide can happen anywhere. In the Great Depression, people walked close to the curb to avoid being struck by men jumping from office windows.

If you happened on someone who was suicidal, what would you do? How would you feel if you were the last person who talked with someone who suicided? Experts estimate about a third do **not** give any signal beforehand. Those who do may not send clear signals. Even experienced mental health professionals can miss clues. Here are signal behaviors, but it's very rare anyone shows all of them.

1. Giving away prized possessions

2. Change in hygiene

3. Depressed more than usual (can seem stupid, inept, or accident-prone)

4. Personality or behavior change (mood swings, irritability, etc.)

5. Social withdrawal, especially from fun pastimes

6. Recent loss or shock (job, property, death of loved one, or a pet)

7. Increased alcohol or drug abuse

8. Increased risk taking or aggressive behavior

9. Thinks about death directly (talk, writing) or indirectly (reading, movies)

10. Has the means to do it and it's lethal

11. Previous serious attempts

12. Suicide of family member, loved one, or role model such as a popular leader or entertainer

SUGGESTIONS

1. *Consider any reference to suicide serious.* *Ask directly* so the point can't be missed.

2. *Be yourself.* You don't have to be a mental health professional or have all the answers. It's OK to be upset, even cry – it shows caring.

3. *Don't preach* ("count your blessings … you have so much to offer"). Some suicides are by impulse and what you think is reassuring could backfire if the person is "tired of hearing it."

4. *Self-disclosure* can help. If you've ever felt depressed and wondered if it was worth living, share it. It can help a depressed person realize they're not alone, others have felt the same but did not act on it. It's been said "suicide is a permanent solution to a temporary problem."

5. *Help provide a safety net.* Mention loved ones, clergy, local mental health clinic 24-hour helpline, AA sponsor if there is one. Everyone should know that phoning 911 gets help quickly and anyone who feels like harming themselves can go to any hospital ER for help. Hospital staff and police routinely contact local mental health services trained to handle such cases. Know your local mental health clinic 24-hour hotline

SKILL BUILDERS

1. *Therapy shopping list.* Which of the therapies would be best for you? Why?

2. *Applied therapy.* Go over the major features of solution-oriented therapy. How can you use them in your daily life?

3. *Suicide prevention.* Imagine you are confronted with a suicidal person. What you say? What would you do? Mentally rehearsing it will help if you're ever in such a situation.

4. *Coping with stress.* How many of the *suggestions* given do you use? Which *don't* you use? Are you able to choose one that is most appropriate to a situation? Why not develop the skill to do so?

5. *Wellness.* How many of the *wellness tips* on page 104 do you use? Which do you especially like? Enjoy them more! Which are you not doing? Why not?

6. *Humor.* To develop your sense of humor, watch more comedies on TV, read more humor in books and articles, check out cartoons, and listen to (clean) jokes. Apply more humor to your daily life by thinking of something funny each day, and if there's nothing funny that day how could it have become funny? Focus only on the positive, not humor at someone's expense or that is negative, cynical, or destructive.

PARTING THOUGHTS

To look up and not down

To look forward and not back,

To look out and not in,

and to lend a hand.

-- Edward Everett

I ain't what I wanna be;
I ain't what I oughhta be;
I ain't what I'm gonna be, but
I sure as hell sin't what I used to be!
-- Alaska sourdough's credo

USEFUL ADDITIONAL READING

Benson, H. (1984). *Beyond the relaxation response*. New York: Harper and Row.
Brill, A.A. (Ed) (1938). *The basic writing of Sigmund Freud*. New York: Modern Library.

Campbell, J. (1972). *The portable Jung.* New York: Viking.

Francker, R. (1973). *Psychoanalytic psychology.* New York: Norton.

Cross, J. & Cross, P.B. (2005). *Knowing yourself inside out for self-direction.* Berkeley CA: Crystal Publications,

Gray, J. (1992). *Men are from Mars, women are from Venus.* New York: Harper Collins.

Fromm, E. (1951). *The forgotten language.* New York: Rinehart.

Horney, K. (1942). *Self-analysis.* New York: Norton.

Keirsey, D. & Bates, M. (1978). *Please understand me Character and temperament types.* Del Mar CA: Prometheus Nemesis.

LeShan, L. (1974). *How to meditate.* New York: Bantam.

MacHovec, F.J. (2005). *Light from the East.* Berkeley CA: Stone Bridge Press.

MacHovec, F.J. (2007). *Divine spark: spiritual intelligence (SI) in you and the universe.* www.lulu.com

MacHovec, F.J. (2007). *Buddha, Tao, Zen: Mystic triad.* www.lulu.com

Maslow, A.H. (1971). *The further reaches of human nature.* New York: Viking.

Meichenbaum, D. (1987). *Coping with stress.* Facts on File.

Nye, R.D. (1992). *Legacy of B.F. Skinner.* Pacific Grove CA: Brooks Cole.

O'Hanlon, W., & Weiner-Davis, M. (1989). *In search of solutions.* New York: Norton.

Peale, N.V. (latest). *The power of positive thinking.* Pawling NY: Center for Positive Thinking.

Rogers, C. (1980). *A way of being.* Boston MA: Houghton-Mifflin.

Selye, H. (1978). *The stress of life.* New York: McGraw Hill.

Sheehy, G. (1977). *Passages.* New York: Bantam.

Watzlawick, P., Weakland, J., & Fisch, R. (1974). *Change.* New York: Norton.

NAMES INDEX

SUBJECT INDEX

OTHER BOOKS
by
Frank MacHovec

Light from the East: A gathering of Asian
   wisdom. Berkeley CA: Stone Bridge
   Press

From www.lulu.com

Lead and manage: Four cornerstones

Divine spark: Spiritual intelligence (SI)
   in you and the universe

Buddha, Tao, Zen: Mystic triad

Pocket I Ching

Pocket Tao

Pocket Buddha

www.ingramcontent.com/pod-product-compliance
Lightning Source LLC
Chambersburg PA
CBHW051812040426

42446CB00007B/641